TERRIFIC GIFTS TO MAKE AND GIVE

DONNA LAWSON

Illustrations by Christine Randall

D1575124

SCHOLASTIC BOOK SERVICES

New York Toronto London Auckland Sydney Tokyo

ISBN 0-590-30885-8

12 11 10 9 8 7 6 5 4 3 2 1   11   9/7 0 1 2 3 4/8

Printed in the U.S.A.   06

CONTENTS

Introduction 5
1. Silly Sneakers 7
2. Frog Prince T-Shirt 10
3. Hanky Top 13
4. Fancy-Schmancy Denim Hat 15
5. Recycled Mittens 17
6. Jiffy Reversible Belt 19
7. Swifty Suspenders 22
8. Braided Belt 24
9. Bubblegum Necklace 26
10. Big Bead Necklace 29
11. Beautiful Junk Bracelet 31
12. Eve's Apple Pin 33
13. Stuffed Heart With A Pocket In It 37
14. Kiss Pillow 40
15. Scented Sleep Pillow 44
16. Balsam Sachet 47
17. Calico Wreath 49
18. Appliqued Pillowslip 54
19. Bandana Quilt 58
20. Sweet Dreams Light Switch 63
21. Dried Flowers in A Basket 65
22. Art Deco Frame 68
23. Denim Paperback Book Cover 73
24. Crocheted Checker Set 76
25. Decorated Egg 80
26. Lip Bank 83
27. Impossible Puzzle 87
28. Eyeglass Lens Pin 89
29. Stitches 90
30. Transferring Designs 94
31. Wrapping It Up 95

Introduction:

WHAT HAVE WE HERE?

Not potholders, or aprons, or any of the corny old gifts to make you're used to getting in this kind of book. No, here you get presents as sophisticated as the ones you see in boutiques and department stores but usually can't afford. Big red satin stuffed lips, an Art Deco mirror, a puzzle plotted to drive anyone wild — they're all in these pages.

Some of the gifts, like the braided belt, can be whipped up in minutes. Others, like the beautiful junk bracelet, take a little longer. But all are fairly quick and inexpensive to make.

Sweet smells play a role too. There's a sleep pillow stuffed with lulling herbs, a wreath that smells like Christmas.

Some of the gifts have built-in messages. A heart-shaped pillow with a pocket in it holds a note saying "I love you." A T-shirt reminds the wearer that "You Have to Kiss a Lot of Frogs before You Meet a Handsome Prince."

Everyone gets a gift in this book. Dad, a crocheted checker set. Mom, dried flowers in a basket. Your sister, a big bead necklace. And your favorite boyfriend gets a pair of recycled mittens.

And, of course, there are the silly sneakers: a tortoise on one foot, the hare losing the race on the other. And lastly you have a bunch of ways to prettily package your presents.

Happy gift-giving!

One

SILLY SNEAKERS

What could be sillier than playing out Aesop's fable on a pair of sneakers? But here it is: the tortoise on the left, the hare on the right. Of course, if one bolts out ahead of the other,

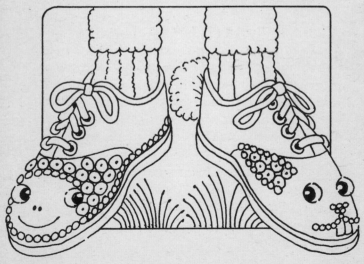

the wearer will be in trouble. But we know that won't happen. Instead the wearer will be constantly reminded that the slow steady one gets there faster than the one who fits and starts.

What You'll Need

plain white sneakers
pencil
textile paint (about $3.00 for six small jars)
inexpensive paint brushes
black waterproof magic marker
moveable button eyes (from crafts store)
Elmer's Glue
large and small sequins
white yarn
a small piece of felt
black shoelaces

Begin by sketching a rabbit onto one sneaker, a turtle onto the other. [Editor's note: drawing of side and front view of each.] With the black magic marker black in the white rubber edge around shoe soles. *For the turtle:* Paint shell patches brown with a black marker line around each. Make the face green; smile red. Everywhere there is a black line glue on a string of black sequins. Line up more around the top of rubber edge. Fill in brown shell areas with green dime-size sequins. For a turtle tail cut out a small triangle of black or green felt and glue to sneaker back.

The rabbit sneaker is painted gray, except for the pink inside the ears, and the teeth which are left white. The ears are outlined in black. A large pink sequin is sewn on for the nose. Then both the nose and the mouth are outlined in black sequins. For the final touch, a white pom-pom is glued on for a tail. *To make the pom-pom* wrap yarn around three middle fingers. Remove yarn from fingers. Then knot a strand of yarn around the center of the loops. Clip loops of yarn on each side of the knot and fluff up ends.

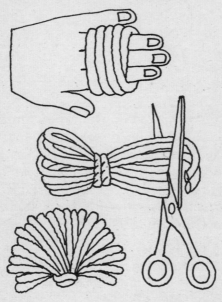

Two

FROG PRINCE T-SHIRT

Every girl needs to be reminded that You Have to Kiss a Lot of Frogs Before You Meet a Handsome Prince. Can anyone not love this gift of good advice?

Materials

white T-shirt
newspapers
blue, green, red, chrome yellow, black
  permanent magic markers
stencils (buy at dime store)
seamstress transfer paper
pencil

First, work out the positioning of your letters on paper. Then, put an ample padding of newspapers inside T-shirt to keep magic markers from staining back. Place stencil on T-shirt and *very lightly* color each letter blue. Note that pressing down too hard makes the color bleed. Draw red lips, and outline them in black. Enlarge frog using grid method on page 94. Then place frog drawing over seamstress transfer paper. And with a pencil, trace over it so it transmits to the garment below. Outline frog's body and eyes with black. Make the mouth red, the pupils black. The rest of the eye remains white. Color his body green; his crown chrome yellow. And once you've worn the T-shirt wash it in cold water to keep colors fast.

Three

HANKY TOP

Look for the frilliest hankies you can find. Scalloped edges give the best effect. Lace edging is nice, too. Romantic prints or luscious embroidery really does it up!

Materials
5 pretty hankies, each a foot square
¼" elastic to fit chest measurement
4 eight-inch pieces of ribbon

(A) Sew three hankies together with scallops or lace on the outside. Take chest measurement

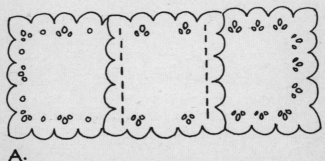

A.

to get length for elastic. (B) Stretching elastic as you sew, gather up fabric. (C) Fold two re-

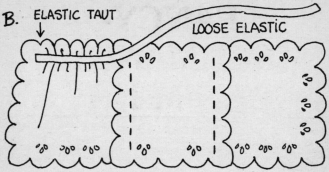

maining hankies into triangle shapes and stitch against both inside seams and again 4" from

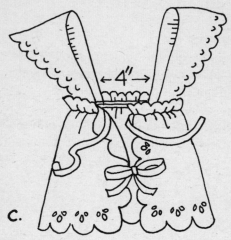

front opening. Sew ribbon ties to both sides of opening. Top can be worn two ways—tied in the front or at the back.

Four

FANCY-SCHMANCY DENIM HAT

Take an ordinary denim hat and make it extraordinary by stitching lace around the crown. Add flower and ribbons to really do it up. Of course, you don't have to stop here. Put beads, rhinestones, stickpins, and feathers on it too, if it suits your fancy schmancy.

What You'll Need
   1 stitched denim hat (from the dime store)
   ½ yard pre-gathered lace
   flowers, ribbons, feathers, etc.
   thread to match

Five

RECYCLED MITTENS

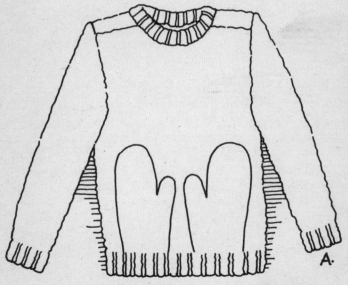

This method is so much quicker than knitting. Just cut your mittens from a bulky old sweater. Then sew colorful yarn patterns onto them.

What You'll Need

a sweater
thread to match
contrasting yarn

(A) Using ribbing for wrists, cut a pair of mittens to fit your hands. Right sides together stitch raw edges using a tight stitch. Turn right sides out and blanket stitch edges. (B) Use a loose chain stitch to make design on back of mitten. (See p. 90 for stitches.)

Six

JIFFY REVERSIBLE BELT

They cost so little to make you can get a dozen going at a time. The ribbons used must be slick for the best bonding effect. Velvets won't do. But even so, your choice is infinite. And making them up is breezy and fun.

Materials

> 2 kinds of ribbon (long enough to go around your waist twice loosely)
> Stitch Witchery® bonding net strip (at dime store)
> 2 D-rings
> thread to match

(A) Bond two pieces of ribbon together fol-

lowing directions on the Stitch Witchery®
package. If the width of bonding tape is too
wide, cut it narrower to fit between the ribbons.

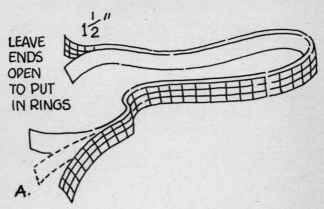

Leave about 1½" free on one end. (B) Use
D-rings (found at notions departments) or some

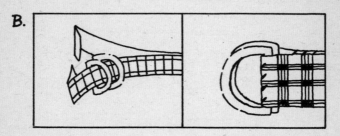

type of a closing to fit width of belt. Turn back
ends of ribbon and slip in D-rings. Then stitch

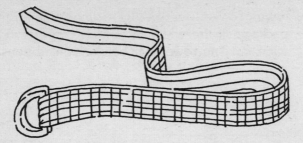

opening closed by hand. Cut off belt as long as you want it. It won't fray because of the bonding.

Seven

SWIFTY SUSPENDERS

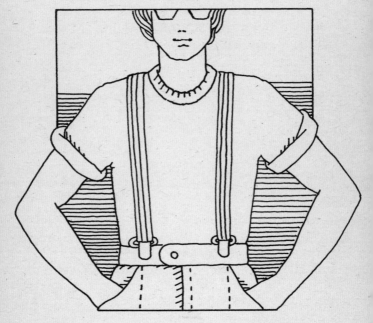

Make a snappy gift for your boyfriend, girlfriend, or your dad. Suspender elastic comes in many widths and varieties, conservative to flashy. Something for everyone. Even slip in a pair for yourself.

You'll Need

suspender elastic (get it at a notions counter)
fasteners in a size to match
needle
matching thread

Measure to get length, plus enough to cross in back. Sew attachments to each one of elastic. Stitch at back cross point.

Eight

BRAIDED BELT

Here's another belt to make in a flash. Make two or three in a variety of colors to wear at one time and package them all together.

You'll Need

3 different colors of cording, measuring circumference of your waistline plus about 16 inches. Look for the cording in notions and sewing departments.

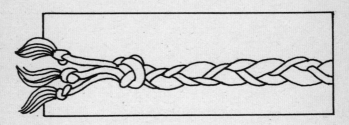

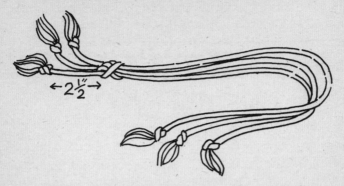

Knot each end of the cording. Then knot the three cords together about 2½″ in from the end. Begin to braid and continue until you come to 2″ from the other end. Then make another knot.

Nine

BUBBLEGUM NECKLACE

Almost anything can be strung into a necklace, even bubblegum. Spray the gum with fixative to keep colors fast, mix with tassels and other beads, or serve it up plain like this one.

Materials

16 big pieces of round bubblegum (buy at the dime store)
53 small pieces of round bubblegum
dental floss (2 yards)
a strong needle
fishing line (3 yards)
crystal clear glaze (or any acrylic fixative)
metal ring clasp

Thread a two-yard strand of dental floss and string bubblegum onto it. (A) Tack up between

SPRAY BUBBLEGUM 1" APART

two points. Separate the bubblegum (about 1"
apart). Spray with fixative and let dry for about
12 hours. Don't spray on a damp day or it won't
dry evenly. Keep the strung floss away from
plastics as they will adhere to each other like
magnets. Take the floss down and unstring it.
(B) Next, double a three-yard strand of fishing

KNOT A METAL RING CLASP TO CENTER

line and knot a metal ring clasp to the middle of
it. (C) Using bubblegumlike beads, string them
onto line. Alternate colors and sizes according
to your taste. String 33 pieces of bubblegum on

the top length of line, and 36 on the bottom.
Then bring both lengths together and attach
remaining clasp. (D) Twine one thread around

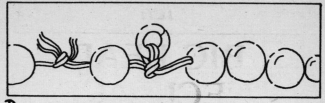

D. FISHERMAN'S KNOT

the other several times and pull tight (in a fisherman's knot) to keep from slipping. To hide loose piece of line push it back through one of the end beads.

Ten

BIG BEAD NECKLACE

Playful, colorful — that's what this is.

To make it, you'll need

> 6 big wooden beads
> 6 small glass beads
> 2 small feathers (3⅓")
> rawhide strip (30" long)
> 2 strips of cord

(A) Double cord and with a double slip knot

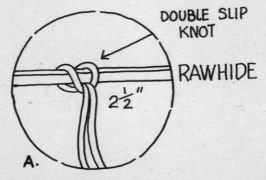

DOUBLE SLIP KNOT

RAWHIDE

2½"

A.

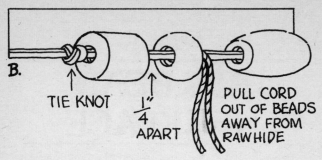

B.

TIE KNOT $\frac{1''}{4}$ APART

PULL CORD
OUT OF BEADS
AWAY FROM
RAWHIDE

tie each onto rawhide about 2½" from center. (B) String large wooden beads onto rawhide, so that they are about ¼" apart. Tie a knot in rawhide at the end of each bead to hold in place. Pull cords out of beads and away from rawhide so they hang in even lengths (they may be partially covered by large beads at this point). (C) String three small glass beads onto cord, then knot a feather at each end.

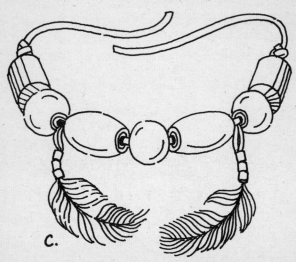

C.

Eleven

BEAUTIFUL JUNK BRACELET

Everything but the kitchen sink goes on this. You can even gear it to the person's personality you're giving it to. If she is a heart freak, hunt down every heart and heart-related object to glue on the bracelet. Do the same for cat lovers.

FELT→

PAPER CLIPS

Or fill beads, buttons, studs in around a doll's face (like the one below). The idea is to make the final product absolutely glittery with jazzy junk.

Materials

> metal bracelet (1¾" to 2" wide)
> pieces of felt
> needle and thread
> Bond 527 craft cement (at paint, hardware, craft and dime stores)
> a small rubber doll's head (from crafts or dime store)
> various large and small ornaments — buttons, studs, beads, sequins, stained glass, broken ceramic, plastic flowers, etc.

To glue objects directly to bracelet they must be flat. You will probably have to trim down doll's head in back to flatten it. Glue it to the center of the bracelet. (A) Buttons which are not flat in back and studs which have prongs must be attached to felt. Then, felt is glued to bracelet, with paper clips around its edges until glue takes hold. (B) Fill in with flat pieces until entire surface is covered.

Twelve

EVE'S APPLE PIN

A tempting gift. Plump red satin, and sweet to look at, if not to taste.

You'll Need

red satin, two 5"x5" pieces
brown satin, two 2"x2" pieces
cardboard to make apple pattern
red and brown thread to match
polyester batting
needle
small bottle of white poster paint
seamstress transfer paper
pencil

(A) Trace apple drawing. (B) Give it a ¼" seam allowance. (C) Then trace around this pattern onto reverse side of red satin. Mark the

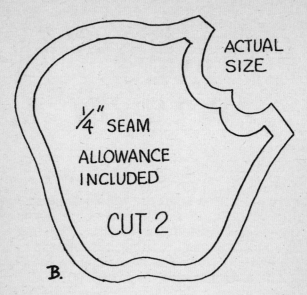

ACTUAL SIZE

¼" SEAM ALLOWANCE INCLUDED

CUT 2

B.

¼" seam allowance. Then, cut out two apple pieces. (D) Stitch together, leaving a ½" opening at top in which to insert stem. Leave a 1"

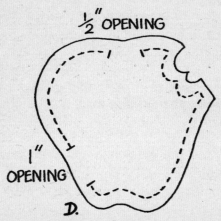

½" OPENING

1" OPENING

D.

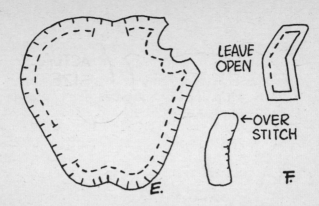

LEAVE OPEN

←OVER STITCH

E.

F.

opening at side. (E) Cut slashes in outside edges to ease it when turning right side out. (F) Cut stem about the size of one shown. Face to face, stitch top and one side of stem. Then turn right side out and overstitch the open side opening. (See stitches, page 90). (G) Insert stem into top opening of apple and secure with stitching. Also stitch closed opening. Now fill

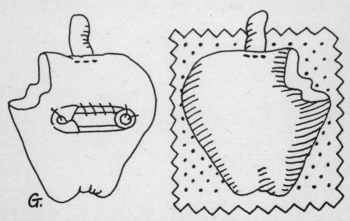

G.

apple with small bits of stuffing until it takes the shape you want. Fold in ¼" seam at opening and overstitch closed. Fill in "bite" with a little white poster paint. For a fastener, stitch a small safety pin to back.

Thirteen

STUFFED HEART WITH A POCKET IN IT

Send a fat pink heart with a little pocket in it for secret messages. Then slip a note into it. "I love you," or "You make me happy," or "Let's meet at the movies, my treat."

To make it, you'll need
(colors are optional)
2 pieces of rose-colored felt, 6"x6"
1 piece of pale pink felt, 3"x3"
1 piece of shocking pink satin, 1½"x1½"
pre-gathered white lace
thread to match
needle

silk pink cording, 2'

Elmer's or fabric glue

4 small flower ornaments (machine embroidered)

2 fistfuls of polyester stuffing

From rose-colored felt, cut two 6" hearts. Cut a 3" heart from pale pink felt, a 1½" heart from the satin. (A) Pin lace between two larger hearts and stitch around the outside leaving a 3" space to stuff heart with polyester. Stuff then stitch shut. (B) Spread glue thinly and glue pale pink

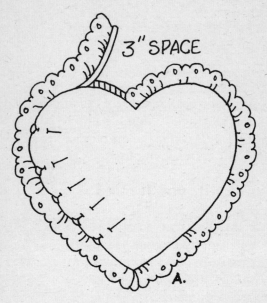

3" SPACE

A.

B.

heart to center of stuffed heart, leaving top open to hold messages. Then glue small heart, cord, and flowers in place. Stitch a bow made from cord to top of heart. Write out your message on a small piece of paper and slip into heart pocket.

Fourteen

KISS PILLOW

Don't let him go to sleep without thinking of you. Give him a big, satiny soft goodnight kiss pillow to prop up on his bed.

Materials

- red satin (1 yard)
- seamstress transfer paper
- tracing paper
- pencil
- thread to match
- needle
- polyester batting

Lips will be about 13" wide at fullest part and 26" long when finished. Enlarge the drawing below using grid method (page 94). Draw in a line where lips would part. (A) Trace lips and cut out paper pattern. Fold red satin in half. Pin pattern to satin (reverse side out) and cut

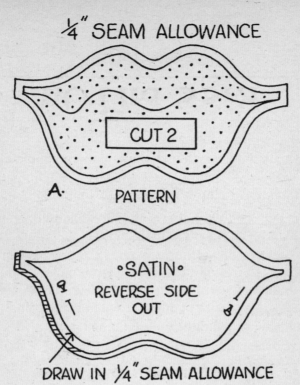

¼" SEAM ALLOWANCE

CUT 2

A. PATTERN

·SATIN·
REVERSE SIDE
OUT

DRAW IN ¼" SEAM ALLOWANCE

around it. Remove pattern and *save*. Draw in a ¼" seam allowance. (B) Stitch together fabric pieces, leaving 5" opening. Then turn lips right side out. (C) Put transfer paper between pattern

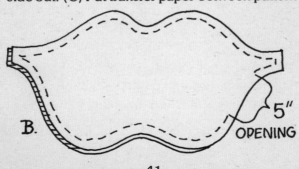

B. 5" OPENING

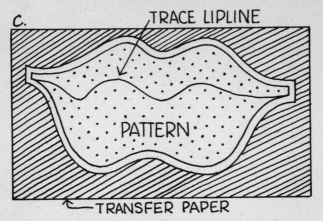

C.

TRACE LIPLINE

PATTERN

TRANSFER PAPER

and face of fabric. Trace over lipline so it transfers to satin lip below. (D) Start in the farthest corner to stuff polyester batting into pillow. As you stuff, every couple of inches, handstitch lipline. Stitch and stuff, a little at a time, until you have the shape and thickness you want. Eventually, the whole pillow will be stuffed with

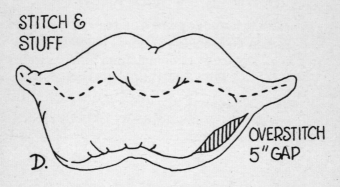

STITCH &
STUFF

D.

OVERSTITCH
5" GAP

42

the lipline stitched. Then fold in the ¼" seam allowance and overstitch the 5" gap (see stitches, p. 90).

Fifteen

SCENTED SLEEP PILLOW

Materials

2 pretty hankies
polyester stuffing
⅜" ribbon trim (about 1 yard)

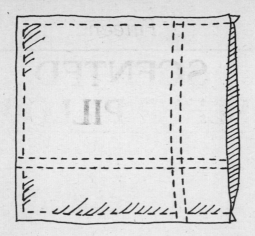

Stitch ribbon to right side of pillow front and back. Then, right sides together, stitch hankies around three sides. The fourth will be left open to fill with potpourri.

Potpourri Filling

Blend:

    chopped peel from a lemon

    2 cups cedar shavings (get a 1 lb. bag from the pet store)

    3 ground cloves

    10 balsam buds (from ends of balsam pine branches) (optional)

    handful of red clover tops (optional)

To this add 2 tablespoons each of:

    nutmeg

    cinnamon

    parsley

STUFF WITH POTPOURRI

Open two flavored tea bags (orange spice works great!) and add to mixture. Add a pinch of ground jasmine. Mix everything together with two cups sawdust (which absorbs and prolongs fragrance) and stuff pillow through open end. Then close with a small overcast stitch (see stitches, p. 90).

Sixteen

BALSAM SACHET

Next time you're near a piney woods look for balsam pine needles. They make a wonderful,

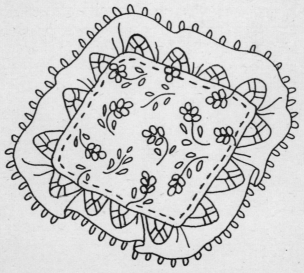

fragrant filling for sachets, stuffed toys or even a calico Christmas wreath (coming up next). Here a small pillow (3½" x 3½") is stuffed with the needles, then edged with lace to make a heady sachet to slip in with your sheets or undies.

LEAVE ONE END OPEN

STITCH RIGHT
SIDES TOGETHER

STUFF WITH
PINE NEEDLES

Seventeen

CALICO WREATH

Before stuffing the turkey, stuff the wreath. And before taking the final stitches, tuck some balsam needles into it so it smells like Christmas.

Materials
12 doubled pieces of calico (5" x 5")
polyester stuffing
Balsam needles (optional)
coathanger
thread to match
needle
2"-wide pre-gathered lace or eyelet, 1¼ yards
red or green ribbon (about 1 yard)

(A) Using wedge-shape (below) as a pattern,

WEDGE SHAPE

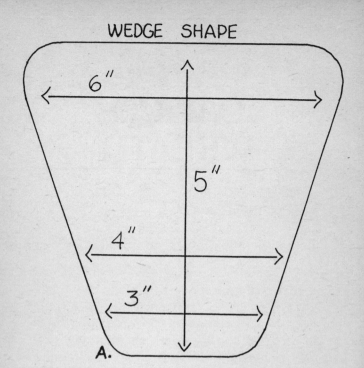

6"

5"

4"

3"

A.

cut 24 calico pieces (sets should match each
other). (B) Right sides together, sew matching

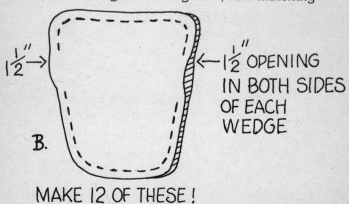

$1\frac{1}{2}$" →

← $1\frac{1}{2}$" OPENING
IN BOTH SIDES
OF EACH
WEDGE

B.

MAKE 12 OF THESE!

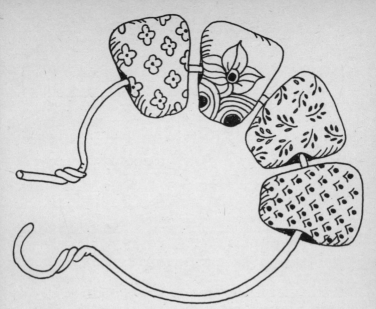

pieces leaving a 1½" opening in the same place on each side. Turn pieces inside out and stuff with polyester. To give wreath a fragrant Christmasy scent put several balsam twigs in-

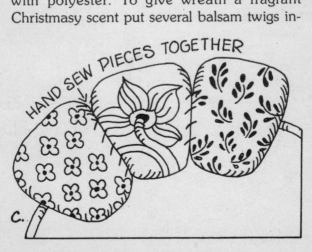

HAND SEW PIECES TOGETHER

C.

TWIST HANGER TOGETHER
HAND SEW TWO TOP PIECES

side. Unwind coat hanger at top, and bend it into a circle. (C) String stuffed pieces around it, running the coat hanger wire through open-

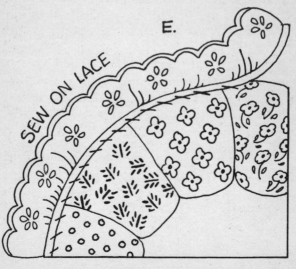

SEW ON LACE

ings. (D) Handsew all but the top two pieces together. When all 12 are on the hanger, twist it back together. Then sew together two top pieces. (E) Attach lace border, by starting at the top and sewing all the way around. (Disguise stitching by sewing from the back.) Attach wide ribbon to top or bottom.

Eighteen

APPLIQUED PILLOWSLIP

Personalize an ordinary pillowslip with a friend's name, and a few pretty calico flowers.

AREA FOR NAME

CUT THROUGH THESE LINES

Materials

    pillowslip
    scraps of printed fabric
    thread to match
    tracing paper
    seamstress transfer paper

(A) Make up your own design or use one below, enlarging it with grid method on page 94. Write name you want to use, in size and thickness desired. Trace design onto tracing paper. (B) Put transfer paper between pillowslip and design. Trace over design transferring it onto pillowslip. (C) Decide what fabrics you want for flowers, leaves, and name. Then transfer them onto fabric. (D) Draw in a ¼" seam allowance. Cut out along this line. (E) Slash several times around the seam allowance. (F) Pin the flower, leaf, or the name onto the

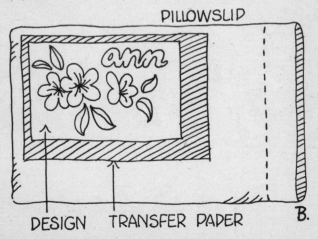

PILLOWSLIP

DESIGN   TRANSFER PAPER   B.

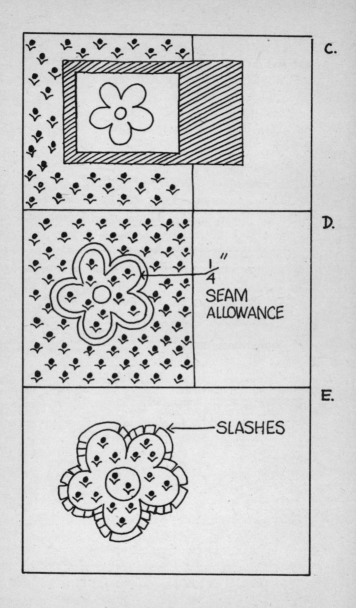

C.

D.

$\dfrac{1}{4}''$
SEAM
ALLOWANCE

E.

SLASHES

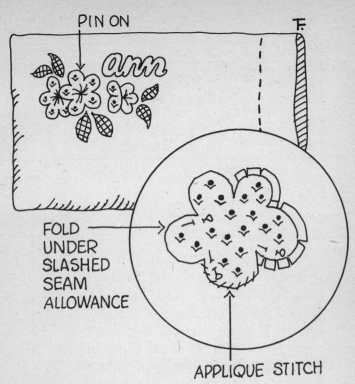

PIN ON

FOLD
UNDER
SLASHED
SEAM
ALLOWANCE

APPLIQUE STITCH

pillowslip. Fold under the slashed seam allowance as you go. Then applique stitch (see
stitches, p. 90). (G) After appliqueing em-
broider flower centers, using a large running
stitch.

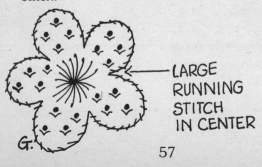

LARGE
RUNNING
STITCH
IN CENTER

G.

Nineteen

BANDANA
QUILT

There's no quicker or more charming way to whip up a quilt. Just six bandanas does it; 16 if you're making a queen size quilt. You can go for the traditional red and blue, alternating them like a checkerboard, or lay out all the newer bandana colors, brown, beige, wine, green, and rust. All in all, it takes no more than three hours to do. Whoever heard of such a thing?

You'll Need
   6 bandanas (red and blue, or a mixture of colors)
   a twin size sheet (or fabric about 4' x 6') in a matching color
   sheets of polyester quilting fill (about 2 yards)
   6 strips of yarn to match, 6" long

SEW TOGETHER

BATTING   SHEET

B.

Lay out bandanas, pinning to follow pattern, as sometimes they are not printed evenly. (A) Right sides together, stitch first two at a

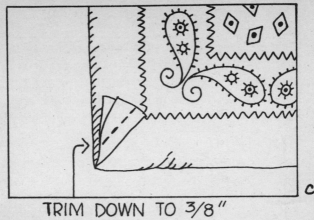

TRIM DOWN TO 3/8"

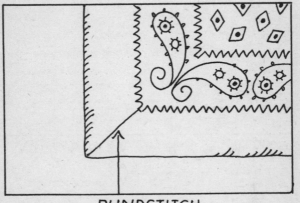

BLINDSTITCH

time, then double pieces until you have a complete top piece. Press. (B) Lay top piece to batting, pin, and stitch around each inner square. Attach sheet, pinning in the center of batting and in several other places. (C) Lap a 2⅜" border around top piece. (Cut away extra fabric.) Mitre corner by pulling up excess material, trimming it down to ⅜″, then turning under and blind stitching. (See stitches, p. 90.) (D) Draw the yarn through the center of each bandana and knot.

D. DRAW YARN THROUGH CENTER

Twenty

SWEET DREAMS LIGHT SWITCH

Here we've given you the moon, plus stars and angels for light switch. But use anything — magazine cutouts, or clippings from a gift card. It will give sweet dreams all through the night.

You'll Need

1 metal switchplate
small can of bright blue paint
box of silver stars
1 gold seal
angel stickers (or cutouts)
crystal glaze spray (or any acrylic fixative)

Spray paint metal switchplate light with the blue so the metallic undercoating shines through. Cut a crescent moon shape from gold

seal and stick to switchplate, along with silver
stars and four angel stickers (or cutouts from
magazines). Spray with fixative, but not on a
damp day or it won't dry.

Twenty-one

DRIED FLOWERS IN A BASKET

Use any flower, grass, tree pod, or budding branch that looks like it will dry well. Feathers are pretty too. Then, get a pretty, cheap basket to hold them.

Gather

branches of mimosa
eucalyptus pods
black locust
honey locust
acacia
dried wheat, oats, and barley
grasses
bent twigs
dried leaves
cattails
pussywillow
goldenrod
hydrangea
cornflowers
molucella
sunflowers
delphiniums
strawflowers
roses

To air-dry pick flowers, foliage, and pods. Tie into small bunches and hang upside down in a cool, dry airy place (like an attic). Flowers with heavy or fragile heads can be dried upright in a jar. Pick leaves off flowers before drying. Note that grasses take about a week to dry; heavier flowers and foliage up to four weeks. Hydrangea and molucellas should be placed in 2" of water and left in a warm room. When the water is gone flowers can be tied, hung, and left to dry as usual. Put styrofoam in the bottom of the basket and poke flowers, twigs, plants, pods, and feathers into it.

Twenty-two

ART DECO FRAME

Early in this century Art Deco was all the rage and now is popular again. One of its earmarks was mirrors. Even mirrors were mirrored. So that's what you have here, a picture frame made with mirrors.

You'll Need

6 small pocket mirrors
3 pieces of sturdy cardboard, 8" × 10"
black enamel paint
black ink
small paint brush
Elmer's glue
Exacto knife
pencil
package of photo corners

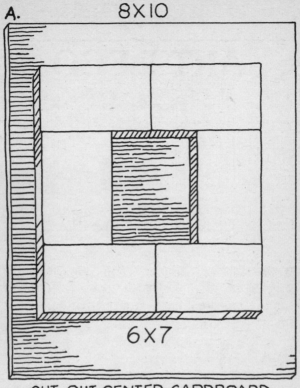

A. 8×10

6×7

CUT OUT CENTER CARDBOARD
& AROUND MIRROR EDGES

(A) Glue mirrors to one piece of cardboard.
(Glued down the mirror will measure 6″ × 7″.)
Let dry for two hours. Using an Exacto knife cut
out center cardboard and around mirror edges.
Center photo on mirror backing, marking

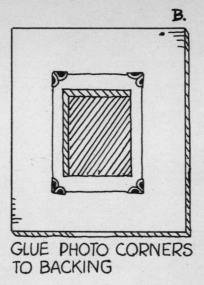

GLUE PHOTO CORNERS
TO BACKING

placement with a pencil. (B) Glue photo corners to backing. (C) Cut a second backing, this one ¼" smaller than the first. Glue it at the top of

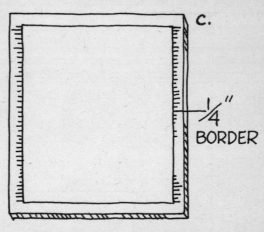

C.

¼"
BORDER

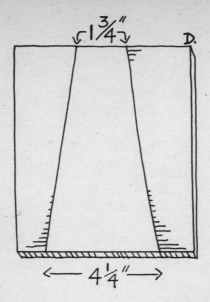

1¾"

D.

4¼"

the first backing. (D) Cut a stand that is the same length as the frame. In width, it is 1¾" at the top and 4¼" at the bottom. (E) Paint Art

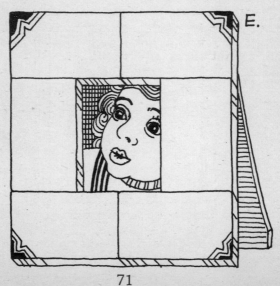

E.

Deco design in each mirrored corner of frame with black enamel paint. Paint cardboard backing with black ink or poster paint. Then place the picture into corners.

Twenty-three

DENIM PAPERBACK BOOK COVER

Choose a favorite book for your friend, inscribe the frontispiece with a special thought, then slip on this zippy book cover.

Materials
    ¼ yard denim
    dime store stencil
    textile paint (a small inexpensive set)
    green thread (or any bright color)
    needle

(A) Fold denim piece over book when closed to get right width, allowing a 3⅓" flap on each side. Pin denim as close to book as possible, then cut it down to 1" on each side. (B) Hand-

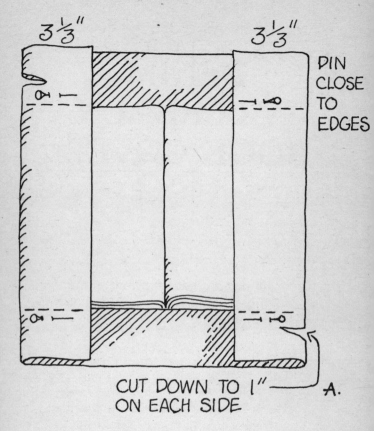

$3\frac{1}{3}''$ $3\frac{1}{3}''$

PIN
CLOSE
TO
EDGES

CUT DOWN TO 1" —— A.
ON EACH SIDE

stitch as close to pins as possible. Cut down edges to ⅜". (C) Fringe about ¼". Using one each red, yellow, green, and blue stencil the word book four times down the front of cover.

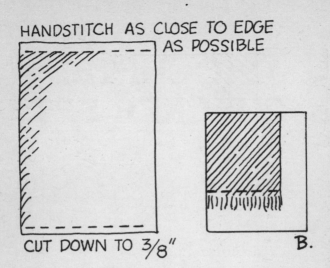

CUT DOWN TO 3/8"

B.

C.

Twenty-four

CROCHETED CHECKER SET

It rolls up and packs in a briefcase, or weekend bag, for Dad or your college-bound brother, or any favorite checker player.

Materials

> heavy rug yarn in 1½ oz. skeins (3 red, 3 black)
>
> J hook

Abbreviations:

DC—double crochet

SC—single crochet

sl st —slip stitch

ch—chain

Each square is 3". The entire board will measure 23" square after blocking. This will include a border of red and one of black.

First row

Red DC in 2nd ch from hook, DC in each ch to the end of ch, ch 1, turn.

Next row

DC in each stitch to end of row (7 DC). Continue for two more rows (4 rows red). Attach black DC in each stitch to end of row. Do three more rows. Continue to alternate in this manner so there are four squares red and four squares black in each strip. Make seven more just like this. Overhand stitch together (see pp. 90). (On any side.) Attach black and SC to the corner, three SC in corner. Continue until you reach where you began. Fasten with a sl st. Now attach red doing the same as with black.

For checkers: ch 4, sl st in 1st ch to form ring. ch 3, DC 12 stitches in ring, sl st to top of ch 3 to join and sl st to fasten. Tuck in loose ends. Checkers will be about 2" in diameter.

If you don't know how to crochet, here's how

Begin with a slip knot on the hook. To chain, pass hook under yarn and catch with hook. Pull through loop. Continue for desired number of chain stitches (A). For double crochet stitch,

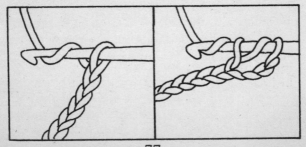

A. B.

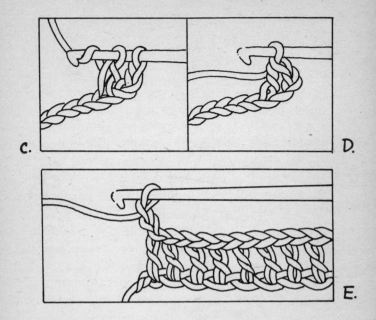

C.

D.

E.

yarn over hook once and insert hook in fourth
chain from hook. Yarn over hook (B) and pull
through two loops on hook (C). Yarn over and
pull through last two loops on hook. You will
now have one loop on hook (D). Continue
across chain (E). To turn at end of each row,
chain two. To add stitches as you go (known as
increasing), work two double crochet stitches in
one stitch...a one stitch increase. At the end of
the project, when you have one loop remaining
on hook, pull yarn over and bring through loop
and break off.

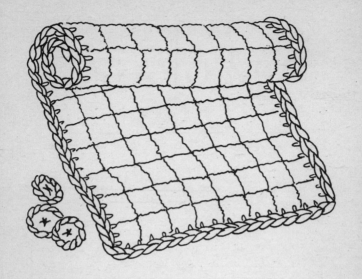

Twenty-five

DECORATED EGG

Use it for an Easter or Valentine's gift or as a Christmas tree ornament. Give it to someone any time just to say, "I like you." It's lovely hung in a window and it can be worn as a necklace if warning is enclosed: "Wear but don't hug!"

Materials

    an egg
    a pin
    decorative seals
    ¼" press type (from art or stationer's store)
    magic markers
    6-strand embroidery floss (about 34" long)
    large-eye needle
    ½" bead
    a tassel

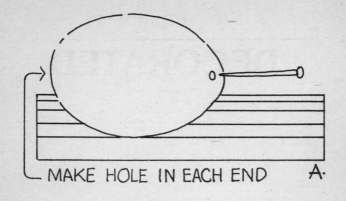

MAKE HOLE IN EACH END   A.

B.

(A) With a small pin, stick a hole in each end of the egg. Blow contents of egg from one end out the other. Let egg dry. (B) Decorate with magic markers, then put seals on top. Use the ¼" press type to print a name, greeting, a saying, or verse. (C) Thread floss through needle. Draw floss through egg. Attach tassel to floss (this will be at the halfway point between each

C.

end). Pull floss back through egg and knot on
other side. String on a bead and knot again.
Then knot again at top of floss. (D)

D.

Twenty-six

LIP BANK

This bank swallows change, or love notes if you wish. And, if you don't make the coin slash it's a candy box (for chocolate kisses!)

Materials

    a round tin box, about 6" across with a red
        bottom half (from dime store)
    a knife and hammer
    tracing paper
    bright blue spray paint
    slick red paper (from art store)
    a single edge razor or Exacto knife
    rubber cement
    Krylon acrylic spray

(A) Hitting a knife with a hammer, make a 1¼" slash in top of tin. Put knife in one direction first, then another, to make slash even. Spray lid bright blue. (B) Cut lips from slick red

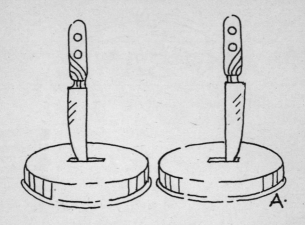

A.

paper. They should be a little less than 6″ across (so they come almost to the edge of the box) and 2½″ wide at the widest point. Use grid method on p. 94 to enlarge lips shown below or

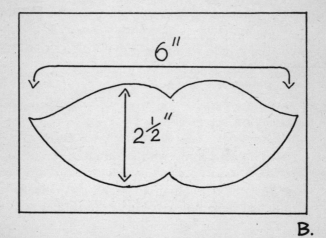

6″

2½″

B.

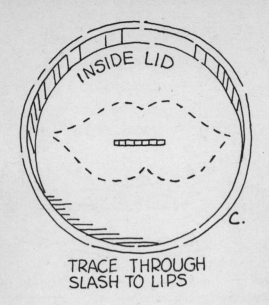

INSIDE LID

C.

TRACE THROUGH
SLASH TO LIPS

cut out your own version. (C) Hold lips on top
of lid and trace slash from under side. (D) Then
cut out slash with Exacto knife. Glue to lid with
rubber cement, lining up slash in paper with

D.

CUT SLASH WITH
EXACTO KNIFE

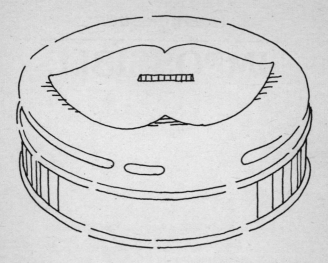

slash in tin. Once lips are glued down use Exacto knife to gently trim back slash. Spray with Krylon acrylic spray.

Twenty-seven

IMPOSSIBLE PUZZLE

Here's a gift to drive your friends wild — a puzzle painted all one color. White is a good choice for the paint, or yellow, or certainly purple. The more pieces the better to create utter frustration. It takes forever to put together, but believe it or not it can be done.

Materials
1 inexpensive puzzle
spray paint
pressure sensitive vinyl letters (½" - 1" size)

Spread puzzle parts out on newspapers, far enough from each other so they don't stick together when painted. Then take a can of spray paint, and completely cover each piece so you have a puzzle that's all one color. Lightly

spray on several coats. Allow pieces to dry between coats, so paint absorbs evenly. Paint the box, too, and label it "Big White" or "Impossible Possible" or some such nonsense, using the pressure sensitive letters.

Twenty-eight

EYEGLASS LENS PIN

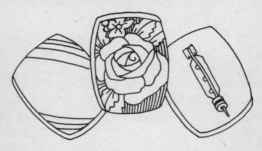

Search the thrift shops for old pairs of eye-glasses. Remove the lens and glue a pretty picture to it and what you've got is a ready made frame for a picture you wear.

Materials

lens
magazine, wallpaper, or wrapping paper
Elmer's glue

Clean the lens well. Put it on top of a pretty picture from a magazine or a piece of wrapping paper and trace around it. Then cut it out. Glue the picture to the back of the lens using a thin coat of Elmer's glue. Then glue a bar pin to the back of the picture.

Twenty-nine

STITCHES

Hem Stitch: Take a tiny stitch (catch only a couple of threads) in fabric and bring needle diagonally through hem. Continue all the way around.

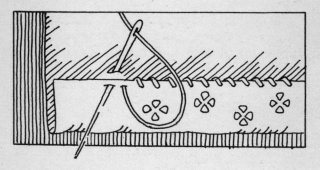

Overhand Stitch: Join two finished edges with small close straight stitches made by bringing needle straight through two layers of fabric. Bring needle over fabric edges from back to front. Then insert needle in front, ¼″ from first stitch, through to back. Then, bring needle and thread over fabric edges from back to front again.

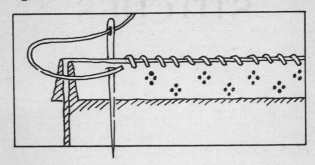

Running Stitch: This stitch is made by weaving stitches evenly in and out of fabric.

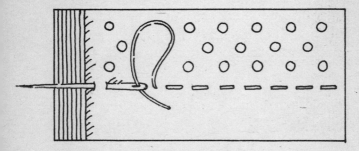

Blanket Stitch: Bring needle up through fabric ⅛" to ¼" from edge. Carry thread over edge, down and up again through starting point. Before pulling thread tight, bring needle under the loop, so it forms a chain of knots along the edge. Each straight stitch is ⅛" to ½" apart.

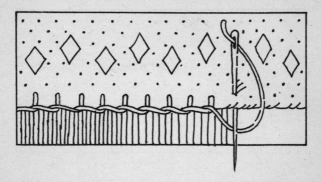

Blind Stitch: This stitch is used primarily to sew down the outer edge of an applique or facing and is almost invisible from outside. Bring needle and thread up from bottom of fabric just outside edge of applique or facing piece. Put needle into applique or facing again

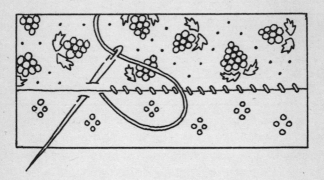

just outside applique or facing edge. Repeat process.

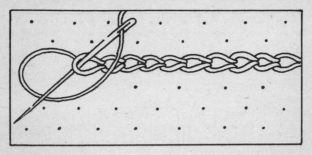

Chain Stitch: This is used to make flowers and other decorative stitches. Pull needle up to right side of fabric. Then, push it back through same hole this time bringing it up ⅛" away. Loop thread around end of needle before pulling it all the way through material. When needle is pulled through it will make a chain. Make next chain the same way by putting needle back into the last hole through which it came.

Thirty

TRANSFERRING DESIGNS

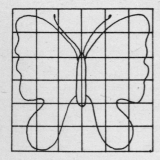 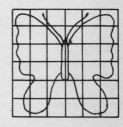

How would you enlarge or decrease a design. Simple: A grid would be used.

A grid is squared off like graph paper. (In fact, for small projects, graph paper works fine.) Measure the design into equal squares. Decide how large you want it to be. Then draw another squared-off box with the same number of squares as the original one, but enlarge proportionately.

Copy design square by square (see illustration).

Transfer design to material by pinning dressmaker's carbon to it and then tracing over the design with a dull pencil or tracing wheel.

Thirty-one

WRAPPING IT UP

Be imaginative in your packaging. Save little brown paper bags to hold small presents. Seal them shut with red notary seals from the stationer's or tie them with yarn (cheaper than ribbon).

Save the Sunday funnies and foreign newspapers. Use stickers and yarn with these, too. Or get colored package twine. Give a second look to all containers before throwing them out. A coffee can sprayed a bright color could hold a T-shirt, the bubblegum necklace could go into an interesting jar with a ribbon tied around its neck, pressure-sensitive letters or a package label can be used on the outside as a greeting card. Boxes can be sprayed interesting colors.

Or you can print your own wrapping paper.

You'll Need

a roll of white shelving paper
poster paints
brushes
newspaper
potato, carrot, onion, cabbage

Paint poster paint colors onto vegetable slices and print them on paper to make interesting-textured designs. Unroll the paper a little at a time. Keep printing until the entire roll is covered. Also try carving designs into the potato—an initial, a heart, or flower—and print them. Or take magic markers and write a name all over the paper (Sue, Jim, David); a holiday —Merry Christmas or Happy Chanukkah—or whatever you wish.

And that, reader, about wraps it up.